SURVIVAL DRINKS

TEAS, COFFEES, NECTARS & SAPS

A unique collection of 21 Wild Drinks for the thirsty wilderness survivor.

DROPSToNE PRESS
Pocket Field Guide: Wilderness Survival Drinks, Teas, Coffees, Nectars & Saps
Creek Stewart

Copyeditor: Jacob Perry

If you would like to do any of the above, please seek permission first by contacting us at http://www.dropstonepress.com

Wholesale inquiries please visit http://www.dropstonepress.com
Purchase this Pocket Field Guide and others in this series at
http://www.creekstewart.com

Published by DROPSToNE PRESS
ISBN 978-0-9985853-9-0

DROPSTONE
PRESS
dropstonepress.com

INTRODUCTION

CHEERS! I wish I were there to raise a kuksa full of Wild Elderberry Blossom Tea as you embark on your own journey of exploring the variety of drinks the wilderness has to offer. HYDRATION is one of the most important aspects of staying alive for any survivor in any environment. Wild water is often made safe to drink by boiling it in many survival scenarios. The wilderness offers thousands of plants, trees, barks, blossoms, mushrooms, roots, and berries that can be steeped in hot water to make delicious, nutritious, and oftentimes medicinal teas and coffee-like drinks. Why just boil wild water to purify it when you can use the plants and trees around you to help that water boost your immune system (and morale) with vitamins, nutrients, antioxidants, and FLAVOR! Boiled water is incredibly boring!

Survival aside, enjoying a fresh cup of wild brew is one of life's simple pleasures. There is nothing quite like picking the leaves from a local plant, brewing it in water, and sipping on the resulting hot tea just before bedding down at night. It's good for the body and soul.

In the world of survival instruction, very few spend much time on wild drinks. However, it is one of those skills that makes living in the wild places much more pleasant. All primitive cultures were connoisseurs of wild drinks. They did this not only for taste, but for medicinal purposes as well. This guide details 21 of my favorite wild edible drinks, divided into three categories: Wild Coffee-Like Brews, Cold Wild Drinks, and Hot Wilderness Teas. Bottoms up!

WILD COFFEE-LIKE BREWS

I hesitate to use the word "coffee" in this description for the beverages I'm about to mention because the only similarity between these drinks and coffee is that a part of the plant/tree is dried, roasted, ground, and steeped with hot water, like coffee. None of them truly taste like coffee, nor are they caffeinated. However, this fact in no way makes these concoctions any less unique, delicious, and suitable for a cold day in the woods.

ROASTED DANDELION ROOT COFFEE

Dandelion Root Coffee

Of these coffee-like drinks, Roasted Dandelion Root Brew has the most coffee-like taste. I've also found it to be less bitter than traditional coffee. Most people can positively identify Dandelion, which also makes this brew a beginner's favorite amongst wild drink enthusiasts.

The unmistakable yellow dandelion bloom

Start by harvesting and washing a mess of dandelion roots. The amount you need will depend on the amount of root coffee you'd like to make. Four roots of an average sized dandelion tend to be plenty for 1–2 cups of drink. The cleaned roots will need to be dried before roasting. This can be done by the heat of a fire (*drying not cooking*) or on a rack in open sun. You can also tie the roots to the outside of your rucksack while hiking throughout the day and they should be just right for roasting by evening.

After drying, chop the roots into pieces so that no piece is larger than ½ inch. These pieces should then be roasted in a pan over the low to medium heat of a fire. The modern oven equivalent of this is 30 minutes at 225°F. It's important to ROAST, not BURN the root pieces. After roasting, they should be a medium brown color, not dark brown or black. Charcoal does not make good coffee.

After roasting, grind the pieces to the consistency of store-bought coffee grounds. This can be done between two rocks or by using any number of modern grinding tools.

I've found that 2–3 teaspoons of ground, roasted root makes a very rich cup of dandy-brew. It can be prepared much like one would make coffee, but oftentimes in the wilderness one doesn't have the luxury of filters or other coffee-related gadgetry. If you're light on fancy tools, then it's best to utilize the Cowboy method of preparation.

Simply place the ground, roasted root into a steaming hot *(near boiling)* cup or pot of water and let steep away from heat for 10–20 minutes *(for fullest flavor)*. This time will allow the grounds to settle to the bottom, and the drink can then be carefully poured *(or consumed)* from the top.

ROASTED CHICORY ROOT COFFEE

Blue/lavender Chicory Bloom

While Chicory is a very common plant in many parts of the world, I've found that it is not actually that well-known. However, when I show someone Chicory for the first time, they almost always reply with, "Oh, that's Chicory? I've seen that before!" Chicory is easy to identify, but as I've already mentioned, BE SURE to positively ID any plants used for food or drink, using multiple field guides and preferably a real person standing on-site with you who has personally eaten or drunk the plant before.

Most will report that the bitter flavor of coffee is an aspect of that drink they would gladly do without. Chicory root has been used all throughout Europe for hundreds of years to cut the acidity of traditional coffee. At times of war in Europe, when coffee was either unavailable or too expensive,

Chicory root was the first and immediate substitute. Roasted Chicory Root Coffee is sold commercially and is considered a boutique, specialty drink. It has a rich, bold flavor that I bet any coffee drinker would gladly welcome in the woods. It has all the flavor without the caffeine and acidic bitterness of coffee. In fact, many are known to cut those qualities of coffee by adding in equal amounts of roasted Chicory root.

The roots are prepared exactly like the Dandelion roots mentioned earlier. The method of preparing Chicory coffee is identical to making regular coffee and can be used in all the available devices or methods. Start with 2 tablespoons of ground Chicory root for every 8 ounces (1 cup) of water and adjust for flavor accordingly.

Note: Another wild plant root that can be used in the exact same way as Chicory is the root from the Burdock plant. Burdock is a biennial, which means it grows for two years and then dies. The second year it produces a tall center flower stalk adorned with small, purple, thistle-like flowers that turn into the famed Velcro-like BURR for which the plant is known.

ROASTED ACORN COFFEE

Acorns – the seed of the Oak tree (too green for roasting)

The seed of the Oak tree is the acorn. Acorns were a staple food source for ALL primitive cultures that lived with Oaks. Acorn, like Chicory, has been used as a coffee substitute domestically and abroad during times when coffee was unavailable or too expensive. Roasted acorns have also been added to coffee to make it go farther when coffee is in short supply.

Considering all the coffee-like drinks listed in this guide, Roasted Acorn Coffee requires the most effort to make. Acorns develop throughout the summer and drop from the tree in fall. If you find one at that time and take a bite, you'll soon spit it back out, due to its extremely bitter taste. This bitterness is caused by tannin. Tannin is a naturally-occurring acid that causes bitterness and astringency. It will also upset the stomach if too much is consumed. This is different from the acid that causes bitterness in traditional coffee.

Primitive cultures discovered that tannins could be leached out of acorns through a variety of methods. One is to soak the acorns *(leaching is accomplished more quickly when the acorns are ground-up)* in the running water of a creek or stream. This was often done in tightly woven baskets, but I've done it in bandanas and t-shirts. The acorns can also be boiled in multiple changes of water, but this is a labor-intensive and resource-consuming process. Ground acorn meal can also be mixed with cold water and left to settle on the bottom of a container overnight. In the morning, the water can be poured off and replaced with fresh water. Once the bitter flavor of the meal has dissipated, after approximately 3 to 6 changes of water *(in my experience)*, it is ready to use. After leaching, the acorns become palatable and can be used as an ingredient in bread, ash cakes, or gruel.

The latter method of leaching is my favorite. However, for the purposes of making Acorn coffee, the preparation varies slightly.

First, harvest the acorns as soon as they have fallen from the tree. Discard any with holes or black markings, as these are a sign of insects, fungus, or mold. **Second,** allow these acorns to dry in the sun for a couple days. This makes shelling them much easier. **Third,** remove the shells from the acorns. Holding the acorn upright on a rock and hitting it on the top with another rock will expedite this process. **Fourth,** crush the acorns into pieces by smashing them once with a rock. **Fifth,** leech them using several changes of water as described in the paragraph above. **Sixth,** once the bitterness has subsided, allow the acorns to thoroughly dry again in the sun. **Finally,** roast the pieces on a pan just like you would for Dandelion root *(mentioned previously)*.

Acorn coffee is prepared like traditional coffee, using approximately 2–3 tablespoons of roasted grounds for a single cup *(8 ounces)* of coffee.

COLD WILD DRINKS

MESQUITE SUN TEA

Mesquite pods soaking in water to make a sweet tea

The Mesquite Tree is a desert dweller that grows primarily in the American Southwest and is very common in Texas and Arizona. At least once a year (*sometimes twice each year depending on rainfall*) it produces a long, bean-like pod. Inside of this pod are Mesquite beans—the seeds of the Mesquite Tree. These pods and beans were a staple food for all primitive cultures who lived around the Mesquite Tree. Despite its bland appearance, the pod is nearly 20% sugar and is extremely sweet. It, along with the beans inside, are packed full of carbohydrates, vitamins, minerals, and protein. While the pods can be eaten at any time, they were typically harvested after they completely dried on the tree and turned in color to a light golden tan. They are best harvested before they fall to the ground, due to the mold and beetle infestation. They can be chewed right from the tree for a very sweet and refreshing trail snack.

Besides being used in a variety of breads and ash cakes, the pods can also be used to make a delicious summer drink. Start by placing dry mesquite beans in a glass jar until it is half full. Next, fill the jar with drinking water to the brim and put a lid on it. Finally, place the jar in the sun for a full day. The sun will heat the water through the glass and leech out the earthy sugars from the mesquite pods. You can pour individual servings or drink right from the jar. There is no need to remove the beans. In fact, they can still be added to other recipes.

MESQUITE POD SMOOTHIE

Mesquite pods will need to be harvested as they would be for Mesquite Sun Tea. However, for this drink, the pods must be ground into as fine of a powder as tools and time allow.

Once dry, the beans are extremely hard and difficult to grind. Primitive cultures ground them using rocks and/or seasoned wooden mesquite pestles. Many depressions in stone, called Metates, can still be found as evidence of how these ancient people used them to grind seeds, corn, and other meals like the Mesquite beans. The photo below is one that I took while filming in the Sonoran Desert. This was one of several Metates areas that I found along a washed-out river bed, called an "arroyo".

Me next to several ancient Metates

Here is a photo of a quickly improvised method of grinding Mesquite pods that I used to prepare a Mesquite Pod Smoothie at a make-shift camp. This system consisted of a rounded grinding stone (*called a "mano"*) and a fairly flat "metate".

Grinding mesquite pods to make a Mesquite Pod Smoothie

After grinding pods, it is usually necessary to remove the large pieces of pith that remain. This includes the sheaths that surround the beans and some other fibers throughout the exterior pod. None of this is poisonous, just bulk that is simply fibrous in nature and is removed to make for the best possible smoothie. If processing in a modern kitchen, this pith can easily be removed by sifting the flour. If grinding primitively, you may find the seeds (*beans inside of the pods)* are too hard to crack. If so, simply discard them or soak to soften.

Once the pods have been ground and sifted well, the resulting Mesquite flour can then be mixed (*like a protein supplement mix)* into a glass of drinking water. Primitive cultures were known to make these drinks very thick. This is because they were likely used as a meal substitute. Personally, I prefer my glass of Mesquite Pod Smoothie to have the equivalent of two handfuls of Mesquite pods mixed inside of a tall glass of water.

PRICKLY PEAR-ADE

Prickly pear cactus with ripe "tuna"

Native to the American Southwest and along the coast from Florida to Connecticut, Prickly Pears are the rosy red fruits of the Prickly Pear Cactus that typically ripen in August or September. These fruits are commonly called "tuna". They are one of the best tasting wild fruits available, but also one of the most armored. Each prickly pear tuna is outfitted with many tufts of hair-like spines, called glochids. They can cause nightmare-ish festering wounds that can last for weeks if you're not careful. I've found that twirling them for a couple minutes over an open flame can quickly singe off the glochids for ease of handling. They can also be carved off with a knife, but it is extremely tedious work. Once these are harvested, they can be made into a deliciously tart lemonade-like drink, suitable for any wilderness gathering.

I've found that two average-sized Prickly Pear Tuna flavor one 8–12-ounce drink nicely. Start by cutting off the ends of the Prickly Pear Tuna. Then, slice it lengthwise. This makes it much easier to remove the tough, outer rind, which you'll want to throw away. You can filet this off with a knife or you can scoop off the flesh with a spoon. Once you have separated the fruit, this can be smashed into the bottom of your cup with a rounded, carved end of any nonpoisonous wood such as pine, maple, spruce, hickory, basswood, or cottonwood. Grind the fruit into a pulp so that it mixes well with water. Finally, pour in drinking water and stir for a tart, flavorful juice. This can also be heated and spiced with cinnamon and cloves (*if you're spending a holiday in the desert and feel festive*).

MAPLE WATER
(MAPLE SAP)

+ its use as a natural simple syrup in a variety of other wild drinks

The widely recognized Maple leaf

Maple Sap is one wilderness drink that I look forward to throughout the year. I'm convinced that this instinctual appreciation runs in my veins as a distant memory from my primitive ancestors who treasured it for so many reasons. Although there are many Maple varieties, most have leaves with five larger lobes. The Sugar Maple can be distinguished from the others with its rounded sinuses (*the valleys between the lobes*).

One of the most unique features of this species is its sugary sap. While the sap from Red Maple, Black Maple, Silver

Maple, Box Elder, Canyon Maple, and Rocky Mountain Maple all contain sugar, the Sugar Maple has them beat. Its sap can be as much as 5% sugar and is the source of almost all store-bottled maple syrups. It takes 40 gallons of Sugar Maple sap to yield 1 gallon of maple syrup after boiling away the water. Maples can be tapped for drinkable sap and do not require filtering or purification. Trees bearing drinkable sap are best tapped in late winter/early spring. However, almost any time frame where the temperature rises above freezing during the day and drops below freezing at night will cause the sap to run. This is due to the change of temperature (*and pressure*).

I can vividly recall when I had my first gulp of fresh Maple sap many years ago. I had hiked deep into the woods on a cold February morning. Around lunchtime, I dug a peanut butter sandwich and small bag of granola from my pack and enjoyed them at the edge of a half-frozen pond. Much to my disappointment, however, I had forgotten my canteen on the kitchen counter, where I had filled it before I left. With no snow left on the ground, I decided to drill a tap hole into the side of a large Sugar Maple tree to see if the sap was flowing enough to collect. Before I could even finish making the hole, sap began to push out from around my blade and dribble down the dusty, gray bark. I reamed out the hole a little bit to clear the wood shavings and placed in a small piece of leaf to wick the sap away from the tree. I then propped my empty granola bag up with a couple of forked sticks and watched it slowly fill—one drip at a time. That one hole produced about 1 cup of sap every 15 minutes, which I eagerly gulped down. It was delicious! It was ice cold, pure, slightly sweet, and incredibly refreshing. After about an hour of waiting and drinking, I went on my way and enjoyed the rest of my hike. Each winter since, I've tapped at least one Maple to collect sap for drinking and it never ceases to amaze and refresh my spirits. "Maple Water" is often sold in high-priced markets as a natural health drink.

Bottled Maple Water for sale

As far as tapping goes, it's very simple. **First,** drill a ½"–1" deep hole into the tree. Be sure it passes through the rough exterior bark and into the sapwood. If the conditions are correct, sap will immediately start seeping from the freshly-drilled opening. **Next,** hammer in a hollow tube, called a spile, to direct sap flow into a container. The spile

can be made from a variety of wild items, including
the following:

- Wild rose stalk *(half or full round)*

- Mullein stalk *(half or full round)*

- Hollowed out Basswood sucker or branch *(the center is
  easy to drill out)* *(half or full round)*

- Piece of bamboo or rivercane *(half or full round)*

- A variety of hollow stemmed grasses

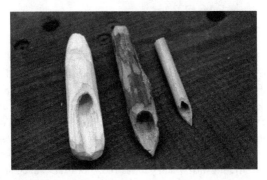

Basswood spile *(left)*, **Mullein spile** *(middle)*, **and River Cane Spile** *(right)*

If the fit of the tube isn't perfect, then pack some mud or
clay around the edges to force the sap through the spile. A
wicking spile can also be made from a piece of leaf or a bark
shaving if a hollow tube is not available. This "wick" can be
positioned in such a way as to wick sap away from the tree
and into a container. Even a small piece of string can work
for this, as it becomes saturated and sap begins to flow
through it.

Carved basswood spile used to collect Maple Sap

Like I mentioned earlier, Maple Sap can be enjoyed "as is", straight from the tree and does not require any additional purifying or filtering. It can also be boiled down to make a thick syrup. However, there is another method of preparation that many have not yet had the pleasure of enjoying. It's what I call a glass of Maple 50/50. This is where you take a given amount of Maple Sap and boil it down until it is roughly half of the amount with which you started. For example, boiling down two gallons of Maple Sap until it is one gallon of Maple Sap. This process produces a slightly sweeter, yet still refreshing, sweet, watery drink. It is especially delicious when chilled in the snow. Maple 50/50 makes an incredible base for any tea listed in this guide—and you guessed it—no additional sweeteners required!

ELDERBERRY BLOSSOM TEA

Elderberry blossom still a couple of weeks away from full bloom

---

Note: Elderberry leaves are poisonous. Use them to help identify the plant only. Elderberry flowers also resemble several very poisonous plants, including Poison Hemlock, so be extremely careful when harvesting and identifying. Be sure to reference two sources for identification and, ideally, be with someone who has harvested and eaten Elderberry before.

Elderberry blossoms make one of the most aromatic teas available in the wilderness. It tastes like flowers. While it must be made with hot water, I prefer it cold (*or at least forest temperature, if possible*).

Start by picking two Elderberry flower umbels *(they do look like little flower umbrellas)* per cup *(typically around 16 ounces)* of tea you'd like to prepare. Depending on your region, you'll find Elderberry Blossoms in bloom May–July, but I've seen them nearly every month of the year in warmer states like Florida. Making the tea is simple. **Start** by bringing your amount of water to a boil, then remove from heat. **Next,** add in the flower umbels and let steep for around 10 minutes, then remove them. **Finally,** sweeten to taste and serve when cool.

Elderberry flowers can also be dried for use all year. Simply pick the umbels and hang them over a cord stretched in a well-ventilated area until dry. Store in paper bags or mason jars and use all year. When dry, use about 1 teaspoon of dried flowers per 12 ounces of water to make this delicious tea.

Elderberry flowers are also used worldwide to make a floral-infused simple syrup that can be utilized to sweeten deserts or other teas. To make it, mix two pounds of sugar with four cups of water and bring to a boil, making sure all the sugar is dissolved. Pour this hot liquid over 20 elderberry umbels and let sit *(covered)* for three days. The result with be a sweet syrup infused with the aroma and flavor or the fragrant Elder-berry blossoms. Remove flowers before use. This syrup will keep for several weeks, but must be canned in a boiling bath to be preserved long-term.

As a final side note, Elderberry Blossoms can also be batter fried to make an incredible fritter. To make, dip a rinsed umbel in a wash of egg and milk. Then, sprinkle with cornmeal until coated. Finally, fry in a thin layer of vegetable oil until golden brown, then salt and pepper to taste. It's an amazing wild treat!

STAGHORN SUMAC LEMONADE
(SUMACADE, INDIAN LEMONADE)

Indian Lemonade made with Staghorn Sumac Berries

The cornucopia-shaped, red berry clusters of the Staghorn Sumac are nearly impossible to misidentify, even though many warn against confusing it with Poison Sumac, which has white berries. In my opinion, the only confusing similarity between the two is the name. However, always reference multiple sources before even thinking about harvesting wild edibles that you've never eaten before.

Staghorn Sumac Lemonade is one of the most unique wild drinks you'll ever make. It's amazing and it is no wonder why it was a favorite drink of many Native American cultures who lived with and near the Staghorn Sumac Tree. The name Staghorn comes from the horn-like branches that are covered in tiny velvet-like hairs. They really do resemble the horns of a Stag in velvet.

Every fall (*typically after August here in Indiana*) I use the berry clusters of the Staghorn Sumac to make a refreshing and simple lemonade-like tea. I've heard Sumac Tea referred to as "Sumacade" and "Indian Lemonade"—and rightly so because the best way to describe the flavor would be as a tangy lemonade.

The sumac berries are best harvested in early fall, before too much rainfall. The tangy flavor is contained in water-soluble crystals that cover the berries—so rain washes it off over time. Thus, do not wash the berries after you harvest them because it is this dusty coating on the outside that will give the drink its flavor.

The easiest way to make Indian Lemonade is to let the berries sit in cold water for 15–30 minutes. This is enough time for the water-soluble acid crystals to dissolve and release that natural, tangy potion that makes your Sumacade. I typically use 2 berry clusters per 1 gallon of water. Because of the hairs and debris present in/on the berry clusters, it is likely you'll want to pour the final product through a t-shirt or bandana before drinking, but other than that, preparation couldn't be easier.

Staghorn Sumac Lemonade is very tart in taste, so I almost always add a sweetener, such as honey or maple syrup. Unfortunately, the berries do not ripen at the same time to make it using Maple 50/50. That would be a very special treat indeed.

GRAPEVINE DRIP

Creek drinking from a Grapevine

What Grapevine Water lacks in flavor, it makes up for in refreshment. There is something about drinking a fresh canteen of water collected straight from the Grapevine—one drip at a time.

Nonpoisonous vines, such as the Grapevine, are an excellent source of fresh drinking water during late winter, spring, and early summer months when the sap is running. Grapevine is the one most people will recognize, but any nonpoisonous vine that drips water when cut is a candidate. There are 4 rules for drinking water from vines: 1) The water should be clear, not milky or discolored. 2) The water should not have a foul odor. 3) The water should have a mildly woody to zero flavor taste profile. 4) No water should be consumed from a vine known to be poisonous such as poison ivy.

There is a trick to drinking vine water that many people have not heard of, and the physics of it is similar to how a gas can works. On the back of most gas cans is a "vent hole". As gas is poured from the can, it creates a vacuum inside of the can, which can greatly reduce the amount of gas leaving the nozzle as you pour. Opening the "vent" allows the can to draw air which, in turn, allows the gas to pour uninhibited. The same principle applies to drinking vines. A crossways notch should be cut into the vine approximately 4-5 feet above where the vine is cut off. This reduces the vacuum effect inside of the vine and allows water to flow out faster and in greater volume.

What about the grapes, you ask? Well, of course you can make a delicious wild drink from those as well!

WILD GRAPE JUICE
(So much better than anything you've ever had at the store).

Wild Grape Leaf

Of any drink listed in this guide, Wild Grape Juice is hands down the most flavorful. This stuff is like a wilderness flavor party in your mouth. It's certainly easier to make this drink in a home kitchen, but it CAN be done in the field as well. It only requires two containers and some fabric (*cheesecloth, bandana, t-shirt*) for straining.

Curling tendrils that are unique to the grape vine

Start by harvesting the grapes, which typically ripen between August and September (*here in Indiana*). All of the juice comes from the grapes, so more grapes equal more juice! The grapes will need to be washed and destemmed. After this is done, place them in a metal pot of some kind and mash them up. You can use the blunt end of a carved, nonpoisonous stick to do this, or a potato masher works perfectly if you're at home. Once they're all nice and mashed, place the pot over medium heat to simmer, not boil. This heat helps to release the juices. Feel free to mash them up while they are simmering. This will help release more juice. Simmer for around 15 minutes or so. Finally, pour the liquid through a cheesecloth (*or bandana, t-shirt, etc. if in the bush*) into another container. This is your finished Wild Grape Juice. Drink hot or cold!

Wild Grapes on vine

If you make this juice, you'll notice it is very thick, almost like a light syrup. You can make this grape flavor go a lot longer if you mix this initial grape juice stock with water. I've found that a ratio of 1/3 Grape Juice to 2/3 water makes a delightful drink that is still very rich in grape flavor.

BULL THISTLE SHOT

Young, second-year Bull Thistle stalk

Bull thistles are ferocious looking plants, covered in sharp spines and hairs. However, they protect something very valuable to a survivor in spring and summer months –WATER. The thick, lush stalks of the second-year *(it's a biennial)* plant can be peeled and eaten like celery. It's best to leave them standing and just work your way around the stalk with a knife until it's all cleared of leaves and thorns – then cut the stalk into sections. After this, they require no further preparation. Simply chew and suck the green-flavored juice for a unique wilderness "drink". I've found that stalks no taller than 18 inches are best suited for this refreshing trail treat. Stalks taller than this tend to be harder and pithy.

Creek sucking on a thistle stalk

If you're feeling ambitious, the stalk and leaves of the Bull Thistle make excellent additions to any fresh pressed juice recipe.

TULIP POPLAR NECTAR SHOT

Tulip Poplar Leaf

The Tulip Poplar *(the state tree of Indiana)*, provides a unique shot of nectar during a very short window *(typically just a few days)* in early spring. The large, upright tulip-shaped flowers *(from which the tree gets its name)* produce and fill with an incredible sweet, syrup-like nectar that bees, insects, birds, and squirrels absolutely flock to when it's in season. One year I even saw a groundhog in the Tulip Poplar Tree at my survival training facility. This nectar is apparently enticing enough to make a climber out of a large ground-dwelling rodent. You'll also find the nectar oozing and dripping all over the leaves and anything else under the tree. If you happen to park your car under a Tulip Poplar during nectar production, a trip through the car wash will certainly be required.

Tulip bloom that serves as the drinking vessel for sweet nectar

If you're lucky enough to pass by a Tulip Poplar tree during this time of year (*or have one in your yard*), the tulip-shaped flower can be used just like a cup to drink the sweet nectar for a sugary, refreshing shot of nature's finest. I think it tastes like liquid cotton candy. They typically only are only about 1/3 of the way full. I've also found that this nectar makes a great tea sweetener. Two of these 1/3-full tulip cups of nectar will sweeten even the most bitter cup of wild brew.

HOT WILDERNESS TEAS

STINGING NETTLE TEA

Hot cup of Stinging Nettle Tea

To some, Stinging Nettle is a noxious weed to be avoided, due to the hypodermic-style needles along its stem that deliver a very itchy, irritating sting. To others, it is a prized wild edible. To me, it is both, as well as the source of one of my favorite savory wild teas. Stinging Nettle Tea is consumed all over the world for its fresh green taste and its many health benefits, including (*but not limited to*) alleviation of prostate issues, intestinal disorders, skin ailments, arthritis, and as an immune-boosting antioxidant. While I'm sure there are many health benefits, I drink it because I thoroughly enjoy it and have grown to crave the smooth, green flavor.

The stem of Stinging Nettle is covered with tiny hypodermic needles

I make my Stinging Nettle Tea the same way every time.
I start by gathering 15 leaves from the tops of young or
old nettle plants. I typically pick 3 leaves from 5 different
plants. I place these leaves in my 16-ounce stainless steel
mug and fill it almost to the top with drinking water. I then
heat the water almost to a boil, then let it simmer for 10
minutes. If I'm using naturally-sourced water on the trail,
I will heat it to a rolling boil and then let it simmer for 10
minutes. I used to always sweeten this tea with one honey packet (which I almost always carry in my kit) but have
stopped sweetening my teas in recent years. Mainly, I think,
because I enjoy and appreciate the unique, natural flavors.

CHAGA TEA

A freshly brewed cup of Chaga Tea

Chaga, *Inonotus Obliquus*, is a slow growing parasitic mushroom that can be found on White Birch Trees in northern climates such as Russia, Canada, Michigan, and America's northeastern states. It is revered by many as a medicinal mushroom capable of anti-inflammatory affects and even preventing/inhibiting/curing cancer. While I don't doubt its medicinal properties, it is also the source of an amazing wild tea.

Chaga mushroom growing on White Birch Tree

Chaga is easy to identify. It resembles a black, crusty mass of charcoal growing in a lump on the side of a White Paper Birch tree. The fact that it looks like charcoal is ironic because it also happens to be a perfectly designed, all-natural fire tinder.

Chaga mushroom must be cut from the Birch tree with either an axe or a saw. It can then be split open and dried. The rusty-colored interior of Chaga rivals char cloth in its ability to catch a spark from flint and steel. Unlike most any other natural tinder on Earth, it will begin to smolder with even the tiniest of sparks. Once a spark has taken, an ember will slowly grow larger and larger throughout the body of the mushroom, and it is nearly impossible to extinguish short of digging it out with a knife or submerging it in water. This ember can be placed into a tinder bundle and blown into a flame for fire lighting. A big chunk of Chaga also makes an excellent vehicle for carrying fire. If kept from too much air, an ember embedded within Chaga can smolder for several hours, allowing a survivor to travel for quite some distance with a ready-made coal for starting a fire.

As an interesting side note, I've found that the smoke from smoldering Chaga fungus also makes a fragrant and effective mosquito repellant when used as a smudge near the sleeping quarters around camp.

Ok, back to making Chaga Tea. I typically make a rustic Chaga Tea that doesn't require grinding or special tools. I start by breaking up dried Chaga into pieces that are roughly 1 inch long on the longest side. It's ok if the black, crusty outer layer is included on these chunks, but be sure to get some of the rusty, amber-colored interior as well. I then bring a pot of water (*roughly 4-5 cups*) to a near boil and place a handful of Chaga chunks inside to simmer for up to a half hour. I normally judge the final product by the color of the water, not by time. I like my Chaga Tea to be a rich, reddish-brown color. Simmering longer makes the tea stronger, which may be more suitable for your taste. You can strain the tea if you'd like through a bandanna or coffee filter, but I never mind drinking Chaga particulates. I will occasionally sweeten with one honey packet, but I enjoy it unsweetened as well.

As far as taste goes, it's hard to describe. Even though it's a mushroom, the taste certainly doesn't resemble mushrooms. It's a flavor that is unique to Chaga. If the word 'forest' had a flavor, I imagine it would be Chaga. It has an earthy flavor that is very enjoyable.

I've used the same chunks of Chaga to make tea up to three times by simmering a bit longer each time. After use, I place them into a mesh bag to hang from my pack to dry until the next time I need them. Once harvested and dried, Chaga can be kept for many months before use and stores very well. And, as a multi-functional survival item (*fire starter*), it is a great mushroom to have around.

MULLEIN TEA

Mullein tea steeped in Birch Bark Cup

Mullein is one of the very few wild teas that I keep at home year-round. And, I only brew it on special occasions. Those special occasions happen to be when I'm sick, have a sore-throat, or feel congested. Many years ago, I read about the medicinal properties of Mullein in an old Appalachian Folklore book, and it suggested to brew a tea from the leaves (*and flowers if available*) for sore throat and to loosen mucus. I decided to try it the next time I fell ill, and sure enough, it worked quite well at helping me breathe and clearing my throat.

Two large, second-year mullein plants in my garden

You can use fresh or dried Mullein leaves to brew this tea, but you must use caution. Mullein leaves are covered in tiny hairs, which can be very irritating to the mouth and throat if you let them get into your tea. Thus, the tea must be strained after brewing or the leaves must be contained in something like a coffee filter to prevent the hairs from escaping. Because I only brew this tea at home, I tie up a couple of Mullein leaves (and a few flowers if it happens to be blooming) inside of a coffee filter and use it this way.

Note: Mullein seeds are poisonous, so do not put those into a tea. These develop in the fall after the plant has bloomed.

I find that the flowers add color and flavor to the tea. The tea ends up being a light amber color and tastes of flowers. It is quite satisfying, even if you aren't sick. Mullein is a biennial, growing a basal rosette the first year and a tall (sometimes as high as 10 feet) flower stalk the next. The covering of tiny hairs on the leaves makes them very soft to the touch, and I suspect this is the reason it also has the nicknames Lamb's Ear and Flannel Plant. Although some people find the hair irritating to the skin, I've used fresh Mullein leaves as toilet paper on many occasions with no ill effects. I've also lined my hiking boots with the foot-shaped leaves before for extra padding, not to mention for their anti-inflammatory and anti-bacterial properties as well. A unique characteristic of Mullein is that the first-year rosette survives through winter, and you can find the pale, green leaves even in the snow.

For brewing I usually wad up one foot-sized fresh leaf and tie it into a paper coffee filter. If the plant is blooming I will add 3–4 flowers as well. If it is dried *(which I also keep at home)*, I will use around two tablespoons full of broken-up leaves. Start by bringing the water to a boil, then remove from heat. Add in the coffee filter containing the Mullein and let steep for 10 minutes. Sweeten to taste.

SASSAFRAS TEA

Three leaves of Sassafras

Note: Sassafras was banned from being used in commercially-produced foods and drugs by the United States Food and Drug Administration in 1960 due to high concentration of a carcinogenic chemical called *safrole* that is present in Sassafras.

Despite the note above, I still enjoy a fine cup of Sassafras tea from time to time. After all, it is this incredibly aromatic tree that flavored early root beer. Its crushed leaves are still the source of the famous Creole gumbo flavoring called filé powder.

Tea is typically made from the roots of the Sassafras tree. They are most flavorful in winter, when all of the nutrients are being stored below ground. To make tea, simply boil 2–4 one inch sections of Sassafras root no larger than the diameter of your pinky finger in water for a few minutes, until the water color is a light amber brown/red. You'll soon find out why root beer became so popular!

BASSWOOD BLOSSOM TEA

Basswood leaves and seeds

Not only are young basswood leaves one of my favorite wild greens in spring, but a hot tea made from the fragrant blossoms is one of my favorite teas in early summer as well. Like the tea made from Elderberry Blossoms, Basswood Blossom Tea also tastes and smells like flowers. Bees flock to the Basswood flowers for nectar. After having my first cup of Basswood Blossom Tea, I could see why. The flowers, when steeped in hot water, produce an incredibly flavorful and relaxing hot tea.

The ratio of flowers to water is roughly one teaspoon of flowers per cup *(8-12 ounces)* of water. I typically use two flower clusters for one cup of tea, but this can be adjusted based on your own personal taste. **Start** by bringing water to a boil, then remove from heat. **Next,** add in freshly-picked Basswood flowers and steep for 5-6 minutes. The color of the water will change only slightly, but you'll quickly smell the fragrant aroma upon steeping. Basswood Blossom Tea is especially delicious when sweetened with Basswood Blossom Honey, which is the honey sourced from bees that feed on the nectar of nearby Basswood trees.

Basswood Blossom Tea is known for calming the nerves. It is also packed with many antioxidants, which makes it a great hot drink if you are feeling under the weather. I've found it to be very soothing for heartburn and even a headache or two. It's not only flavorful, but good for the body as well! Many times, I've made the tea utilizing only materials from the Basswood tree. Sap is sometimes running at the time the Basswood flowers are around. I will hollow out a small Basswood branch as a spile *(see photo under Maple Water)* and tap the tree for a few cups of Basswood sap. Then, I will boil this sap as the water for my Basswood Blossom Tea. While the water is coming to a boil, I'll sit under the shade of the tree and nibble on young Basswood leaves. It doesn't get much better than this. There's so much more to the

Basswood tree than tea. For details about all of the survival uses of Basswood, consider my POCKET FIELD GUIDE titled SURVIVAL TREES: VOL I.

PINE NEEDLE TEA

A freshly brewed cup of Pine Needle Tea, rich in Vitamin C

Pine trees are an evergreen (*year-round, green needles*) and a conifer (*cone-bearing*), and I often hear people call all evergreens (*including spruce, cedar, and hemlock*) Pine trees. This is not the case. Pine trees grow needles in clusters that bear anywhere between 2–5 needles. The number of needles per cluster, length of needles, size of tree, type of cone, and style of bark are all used to help differentiate between species of Pine. I've had Pine Needle Tea from different species of Pine all over North America, and they all essentially taste the same – like Pine smells!

There is no other drink that tastes and smells like the forest as much as Pine Needle Tea. It is probably the wild tea that I drink the most often. This is mainly for two reasons. **First,** when I'm in the wild I almost always try to make camp in a grove of pines, and using the needles from the surrounding trees just happens to be very convenient as I settle down and start thinking about a hot cup of tea before bed. **Second,** it is extremely easy to make. It is not only flavorful, but is also rich in Vitamin C, which no one should ever turn away. Making it is simple. **First,** bring your tea water to a boil and remove from heat. **Next,** crush a handful of pine needles and steep in hot water for 10 minutes. **Finally,** strain out needles and drink.

Note: Crushing the needles a bit is important. Pine needles are water-tight, sealed little capsules of flavor. To best release this flavor in your tea, you must bust the exterior shell of the needle. I typically just use the pommel (*bottom of the handle*) of my knife and crush them against a rock or on my little camp cutting board, which I always have with me.

BIRCH TWIG TEA

Birch Twig Tea

The twig tips from the White, Yellow, and Black Birch make one of my favorite cold weather drinks. The unique wintergreen flavor is a standout among most every other wilderness drink. Furthermore, preparation is extremely easy, which is nice for a survivor or hiker on the go. Not only can White Birch provide the delicious and medicinal Chaga Tea, but it bears the entirely different flavor profile of a wintergreen Twig Tea as well.

The hardest part of making Birch Twig Tea is accessing the small twig tips required for flavoring. Once you locate a lower branch where you can access the tips of the twigs, snap off a handful of twig tips measuring about four inches long. Just 3-4 twig tips flavor a cup of water nicely. I typically use a handful of tips when brewing a pot.

To make the tea, bring a pot or cup of water to a rolling boil and remove from heat. Then, place twig tips into the hot water and let steep for 10 minutes. You'll almost immediately smell the very aromatic wintergreen scent. The only thing better than the smell is the taste. Sweeten if desired. Oftentimes, in late winter/early spring, you can tap the Birch for tea water as well! The sap from the Birch is drinkable right from the tree without any further processing. In fact, Birch sap can be boiled down to make a syrup, just like Maple Sap. However, instead of a 40:1 gallon ration like Maple, a 100:1 gallon ratio is required for Birch. Consequently, Birch Syrup is very expensive. But to a traveling wilderness wanderer, the sap and twigs are FREE!

BLACK LOCUST BLOSSOM TEA

Black Locust Blossom Tea

You'll never notice a Black Locust Tree until early spring (*May-ish*) when it's dripping with dangles of snow-white blossoms. These blossoms not only make a delicious tea, but can also be batter fried as a fritter for a filling side dish to any wild meat.

Black Locust Blossoms on tree (*all other parts of this tree are poisonous*)

To make this tea, I typically use a ratio of 2 blossoms (*the entire blossom, not just one flower*) to one 16-ounce cup of hot water. Like many of the blossom teas mentioned in this guide, first bring the water to a boil and remove from heat. Then, steep the blossoms in the water for 10 minutes to make a fragrant and floral-tasting tea. I always eat the blossoms after, which taste like a cross between flowers and peas.

Other blossoms that can be prepared in the same way are those from the Redbud Tree, White Clover, Violet, Red Clover, Dandelion, Blackberry, and Thistle.

Red Clover Bloom

CONCLUSION

Throughout my many years of study and adventure in the wilderness, I've found the most pleasure in the simplest things. A fine mug of hot wild tea next to the campfire before bed is certainly one of my favorites. Whether for taste, comfort, medicine, or sheer hydration, the wilderness provides countless drinking options. While this guide includes some of my favorite wild drinks, it has only begun to scratch the surface of what's available to a thirsty student of the wild places. If you have a favorite wilderness drink, please share it with me by emailing **creek@creekstewart.com**. I just may include it in a future volume of WILDERNESS DRINKS! Look for more POCKET FIELD GUIDES on other survival topics anywhere books are sold.

Remember, it's not IF *but* WHEN,
CREEK

NOTES:

NOTES:

_____

_____

_____

_____

_____

_____

_____

_____

_____

_____

_____

_____

_____

_____

_____

_____

_____

_____

_____

_____

_____

NOTES:

NOTES:

NOTES: